The Power of Discipline

How to Develop Courage and Fortitude to Persevere and Succeed

Author

Daniel Walker, Eddie McKeon

Copyright © 2023 All Rights Reserved

The Author's Note

This book is a trustworthy source of information on the topic. The publisher is selling the book because they are exempt from providing auditing, licensing, or certified services. Request the opinion of a lawyer or other qualified expert.

This document may not be reproduced in any form. Without the publisher's express written consent, copying and storing any part of this publication is illegal. Protected by law.

The reader assumes full responsibility for the consequences of following or misusing any procedures, policies, or guidelines outlined herein. The publisher assumes no responsibility for any losses, costs, or repairs you might incur from using the data contained herein.

Copyright © 2023 by Daniel Walker, Eddie McKeon

Copyright fuels creativity, encourages diverse voices, promotes free speech, and creates a vibrant culture. Thank you for buying a copy of this book.

Book Title: The Power of Discipline How to Develop Courage and Fortitude to Persevere and Succeed

ISBN: 978-1-312-51188-0

Author: Daniel Walker, Eddie McKeon

Contents

Chapter 1 5
The Importance of Discipline 5
   Understanding Discipline 5
   Why Discipline Matters 7
   The Link between Discipline and Success 9
Chapter 2 11
Building the Foundation: Self-Awareness and Goal Setting 11
   Developing Self-Awareness 11
   Setting Meaningful Goals 13
   Aligning Goals with Values 15
Chapter 3 17
Cultivating Courage 17
   Understanding Courage 17
   Overcoming Fear and Taking Risks 19
   Developing Resilience 21
Chapter 4 24
The Power of Focus 24
   Concentration and Mental Clarity 24
   Eliminating Distractions 26
   Practicing Mindfulness 29
Chapter 5 32
Developing Habits and Routines 32
   Creating Positive Habits 32
   Breaking Bad Habits 34
   Establishing Effective Daily Routines 38
Chapter 6 40

Emotional Intelligence and Self-Control 40
    Understanding Emotional Intelligence 40
    Managing Emotions 42
    Developing Self-Control 45

Chapter 7 48
Perseverance and Grit 48
    The Role of Perseverance in Success 48
    Cultivating Grit 50
    Overcoming Obstacles and Challenges 52

Chapter 8 55
Discipline in Action: Strategies and Techniques 55
    Time Management and Prioritization 55
    Creating Accountability Structures 57

Chapter 9 60
Maintaining Balance and Well-being 60
    Balancing Work and Personal Life 60
    The Role of Discipline in Overall Well-being 62

Chapter 10 66
Overcoming Setbacks and Bouncing Back 66
    Learning from Failure 66
    Reframing Challenges as Opportunities 68

Goal-Setting Worksheet 71
Conclusion 74

Chapter I

The Importance of Discipline

Understanding Discipline

Discipline is the foundational quality that empowers individuals to persevere and succeed in their endeavors. It involves consistently adhering to a set of rules, principles, or routines, even in the face of challenges or distractions. By cultivating discipline, individuals gain the courage and fortitude to overcome obstacles, stay focused on their goals, and achieve long-term success.

Case Study: John's Journey to Disciplined Living

A recent college graduate, John struggled to transition into the professional world. He was filled with ambition and dreams but lacked the discipline to turn them into reality. His days were often filled with procrastination, distractions, and a lack of direction.

Recognizing the need for change, John developed discipline as a core trait. He embarked on a journey to understand the importance of discipline and how it could transform his life.

First, John focused on self-awareness and goal setting. He engaged in introspection to understand his strengths, weaknesses, and values. By aligning his goals with his core values, he developed a strong sense of purpose, which drove his disciplined approach.

Next, John realized that cultivating courage was essential to combat his fears and overcome challenges. He began embracing discomfort and taking calculated risks, gradually building resilience and grit. His confidence grew as he faced his fears head-on, propelling him forward.

To enhance his focus, John practiced the power of concentration and mindfulness. He learned to eliminate distractions by setting boundaries and creating a conducive environment for deep work. This allowed him to channel his energy and attention toward his most important tasks, boosting his productivity and efficiency.

John understood that discipline relied on developing positive habits and routines. He created a daily schedule incorporating activities aligned with his goals, such as exercising, reading, and working on professional projects. Through consistent practice, these habits became ingrained, reinforcing his discipline.

Emotional intelligence and self-control played crucial roles in John's journey. By becoming aware of his emotions and managing them effectively, he avoided impulsive actions and made better decisions. He learned to delay gratification, resisting short-term temptations in favor of long-term rewards.

John faced setbacks and challenges along the way, but he persevered. He viewed failures as opportunities for growth, learning valuable lessons, and adapting his strategies accordingly. His ability to bounce back and maintain discipline in adversity propelled him closer to his goals.

As John sustained his discipline, he discovered the importance of balance and well-being. He recognized that caring for his physical and mental health was essential for maintaining a disciplined lifestyle. By prioritizing self-care, he ensured he had the energy and clarity of mind necessary to persist and succeed.

Through his disciplined approach, John witnessed remarkable transformations in his life. He achieved his professional goals, built meaningful relationships, and experienced a sense of fulfillment. Discipline became the bedrock of his success, empowering him to face challenges head-on and persevere, no matter the circumstances.

In conclusion, understanding discipline is the key to unlocking one's potential and achieving success. By following John's example and embracing discipline in our lives, we can develop the courage and fortitude to persevere, overcome obstacles, and thrive in our pursuits.

Why Discipline Matters

Discipline is a fundamental trait that is crucial to personal and professional success. It catalyzes achieving goals, overcoming obstacles, and leading a purposeful life. Here are some reasons why discipline matters:

1. Goal Achievement: Discipline provides the structure and focuses necessary to pursue and achieve goals. It enables individuals to prioritize tasks, stay committed, and consistently act on their objectives. Without discipline, goals may remain mere aspirations, never materializing into tangible accomplishments.

2. Consistency and Productivity: Discipline breeds feeling, allowing individuals to develop productive habits and routines. When tasks are approached with discipline, they are completed efficiently and effectively. Staying on track and following through consistently enhances productivity and maximizes results.

3. Resilience and Perseverance: Discipline empowers individuals to face challenges and setbacks with resilience. It provides the mental and emotional strength needed to persist in adversity. Discipline enables individuals to stay focused on their long-term vision, pushing through difficulties and returning from failures.

4. Time Management: Discipline is essential for effective time management. It helps individuals prioritize tasks, allocate time wisely, and avoid procrastination. With discipline, individuals can make the most of their time, ensuring that essential tasks are completed, and deadlines are met.

5. Self-Control and Emotional Intelligence: Discipline fosters self-control and emotional intelligence, enabling individuals to regulate their impulses and make rational decisions. It helps individuals resist distractions, temptations, and impulsive behaviors that may hinder progress. Individuals can make choices aligned with their long-term goals and values by exercising discipline.

6. Personal Growth and Development: Discipline catalyzes personal growth and development. It requires individuals to step outside their comfort zones, take on challenges, and continuously improve. Individuals can acquire new skills, expand their knowledge, and reach their full potential through disciplined efforts.

7. Building Trust and Reliability: Discipline cultivates trust and reliability. When individuals consistently demonstrate discipline in their actions, they become known for their reliability and dependability. This enhances professional relationships, fosters trust among colleagues and clients and opens doors for further opportunities.

8. Mental and Physical Well-being: Discipline contributes to overall well-being. By incorporating healthy habits and routines, individuals can improve their physical health, mental clarity, and overall quality of life. Discipline allows individuals to prioritize self-care, manage stress, and maintain a healthy work-life balance.

Discipline is essential to life. It aids in goal-setting, consistency, overcoming obstacles, and personal growth. Specialization unlocks potential and leads to lasting success.

The Link between Discipline and Success

Discipline and success are intrinsically linked, with occupation as a powerful catalyst for achieving significant accomplishments. Cultivating discipline in one's life is vital to success across various domains. Let's explore this link through a case study:

Case Study: Sarah's Journey to Professional Success

Sarah, a young professional, had ambitious career aspirations. However, she realized that without discipline, her dreams would remain unfulfilled. She embarked on a journey to develop discipline as the cornerstone of her path to success.

Sarah understood that discipline would be crucial in managing her time effectively and prioritizing her tasks. She implemented a structured schedule, allocating specific time slots for essential projects, skill development, and networking. Through disciplined time management, Sarah could consistently invest her energy in activities that propelled her toward her career goals.

In addition to time management, Sarah recognized that discipline was essential in building expertise in her field. She committed to continuous learning, setting aside dedicated daily hours to study industry trends, attend webinars, and read relevant books. By embracing discipline in her pursuit of knowledge, Sarah became a subject matter expert, enhancing her professional competence.

Sarah also understood the significance of discipline in maintaining focus and avoiding distractions. She consciously limited her time spent on social media and implemented strategies to resist the urge to engage in non-productive activities during work hours. By exercising discipline, Sarah kept her attention on her work, enhancing her concentration and productivity.

Furthermore, Sarah realized that discipline was vital in fostering resilience and perseverance. She encountered setbacks and faced professional challenges along her journey. However, her discipline-driven mindset enabled her to stay committed, learn from failures, and bounce back stronger. Sarah used discipline to maintain a positive attitude, adapt her strategies, and persist in the face of adversity.

As Sarah continued cultivating discipline in her professional life, she witnessed its direct impact on her success. She received recognition for her outstanding work, earned promotions, and was entrusted with leadership roles. Sarah's disciplined approach instilled trust and reliability among her colleagues and superiors, opening doors to new opportunities and career advancement.

Sarah's case study exemplifies the link between discipline and success. By consistently practicing the profession, she established habits that maximized her productivity, enhanced her skills, and bolstered her resilience. Through her disciplined efforts, Sarah achieved significant milestones and progressed steadily on her path to professional success.

Success requires discipline. It helps people focus, manage time, gain expertise, overcome challenges, and be reliable. Domain helps people like Sarah achieve their goals, reach their potential, and succeed.

Chapter 2

Building the Foundation: Self-Awareness and Goal Setting

Developing Self-Awareness

Self-awareness is the foundation of personal growth and success. It involves understanding oneself, including strengths, weaknesses, values, beliefs, and emotions. Individuals gain valuable insights that inform their decisions, behaviors, and relationships by developing self-awareness. Let's explore the concept of developing self-awareness through a case study:

Case Study: Alex's Journey to Self-Awareness

A young professional, Alex felt unfulfilled and unsure of his career path. He realized that self-awareness was crucial to gaining clarity and making meaningful choices. Alex embarked on a journey of self-discovery and growth.

Initially, Alex engaged in introspection and self-reflection to explore his interests, values, and aspirations. He identified his core values and what truly mattered to him. This process of self-reflection allowed him to understand his priorities and align his choices with his authentic self.

Alex also sought feedback from trusted mentors and friends. He welcomed constructive criticism and actively listened to their perspectives on his strengths and areas for improvement. This feedback provided valuable insights into his blind spots and helped him better perceive himself.

To deepen his self-awareness, Alex incorporated mindfulness practices into his daily routine. He could observe his thoughts, emotions, and reactions without judgment through meditation and self-observation. This mindfulness practice heightened his awareness of his internal experiences, allowing him to understand his thinking patterns and behavior better.

Alex also explored personality assessments and psychometric tools to gain further insights into his personality traits, preferences, and strengths. These assessments served as a valuable framework for self-reflection and provided him with language to describe his unique qualities.

Through his journey of self-awareness, Alex gained clarity on his career goals. He realized his passion lay in a different field than his current profession. With this newfound understanding, he made a courageous decision to transition to a career aligned with his values and interests.

Alex's case study illustrates the transformative power of self-awareness. By embarking on a journey of self-discovery, he gained a deep understanding of his authentic self and made informed decisions that aligned with his values and aspirations.

Developing self-awareness is crucial for personal and professional growth. It enables individuals to make choices that align with their true selves, increasing satisfaction and fulfillment. Self-awareness also enhances interpersonal relationships as individuals become more attuned to their own emotions and better understand the perspectives of others.

In a nutshell, self-awareness transforms people to make authentic choices and live their values. Self-discovery can help people like Alex reach their full potential and live more purposefully.

Setting Meaningful Goals

Setting meaningful goals is a critical step in achieving personal and professional success. Meaningful goals provide direction, motivation, and a sense of purpose. They help us focus our energy and efforts, enabling us to make progress and experience a sense of fulfillment. Here are key points to consider when setting meaningful goals:

1. Reflect on Your Values and Passions: Reflect on your values, passions, and what truly matters to you. Consider what brings you joy, fulfillment, and a sense of purpose. Aligning your goals with your core values and passions ensures that they resonate deeply with you, increasing your commitment and motivation to pursue them.

2. Make Them Specific and Measurable: Set goals that are specific and measurable. Clearly define your purpose and establish concrete criteria to measure your progress. Clear and quantifiable goals provide clarity and allow you to track your advancement, making it easier to stay focused and motivated.

3. Set Realistic and Challenging Goals: Balance realism and ambition when setting goals. While it's essential to aim high and challenge yourself, ensure your goals are attainable within a reasonable timeframe. Setting too far-fetched goals can lead to discouragement, while goals that are too easy may not inspire growth and stretch your capabilities.

4. Break Them Down into Actionable Steps: Break your goals into smaller, actionable steps. This makes them more manageable and helps you create a clear roadmap towards achievement. Each step becomes a mini-goal, and as you

accomplish each, you build momentum and confidence in pursuing the larger goal.

5. Set Short-term and Long-term Goals: Establish both short-term and long-term goals. Short-term goals provide immediate focus and gratification, while long-term goals provide a broader vision and purpose. Balancing both plans allows for continuous progress and keeps you motivated on your journey.

6. Write Them Down and Review Regularly: Write your goals down and keep them visible. This helps solidify your commitment and constantly reminds you of what you are working towards. Regularly review your plans to track progress, make necessary adjustments, and stay connected to your purpose.

7. Consider Different Areas of Life: Set goals encompassing various areas of your life, such as career, health, relationships, personal development, and hobbies. Balancing goals across different places allows for holistic growth and fulfillment.

8. Stay Flexible and Adapt: Understand that goals may need adjustments. Circumstances and priorities may change, and staying flexible and adapting as required is essential. Reassess your goals periodically to ensure they remain relevant and meaningful to you.

You create a roadmap for success and personal fulfillment by setting meaningful goals. They provide a sense of purpose, motivate you to take action, and enable you to progress in the areas that matter most to you. You can achieve extraordinary results and experience a profound sense of accomplishment with clarity and focus on meaningful goals.

Aligning Goals with Values

Aligning goals with values is crucial in setting meaningful and fulfilling dreams. When our goals align with our core values, we experience a greater sense of purpose, motivation, and satisfaction. Aligning goals with values helps ensure our pursuits are authentic and align with what truly matters to us. Let's explore the importance of aligning goals with values through a case study:

Case Study: Emily's Journey to Alignment

Emily, a young professional, was feeling dissatisfied with her career. She realized that her goals were not aligned with her core values, resulting in a lack of fulfillment and motivation. Emily embarked on a journey to realign her dreams with her values and find a more purposeful path.

Emily identified her core values—authenticity, growth, and work-life balance. She reflected on these values and how they could guide her career choices. She realized that her current goals focused solely on external markers of success, such as salary and job title, but neglected the values that truly mattered to her.

Emily set aside time for introspection and self-reflection to align her goals with her values. She considered what kind of work would allow her to be true to herself, foster personal growth, and support a healthy work-life balance. This process helped her clarify her professional aspirations and the values she wanted to honor.

With a newfound understanding of her values, Emily revised her career goals. She shifted her focus towards pursuing a career that allowed her to express her authentic self, cultivate continuous growth, and maintain a healthy work-life balance. She decided to explore opportunities aligned with her values, such as flexible work arrangements, personal development programs, and industries aligned with her passion for sustainability.

Emily also sought support from a career coach who helped her align her goals with her values. Together, they explored different career paths and evaluated how each option aligned with her core values. This guidance provided her with clarity and confidence in making career decisions that were true to herself.

Through her intentional efforts to align her goals with her values, Emily experienced a remarkable transformation. She found a new job in a sustainability-focused organization that allowed her to express her authenticity, embrace personal growth, and maintain a healthy work-life balance. The alignment between her goals and values brought a renewed sense of purpose and fulfillment in her professional life.

Emily's case study exemplifies the importance of aligning goals with values. By recognizing the misalignment between her dreams and values, she took proactive steps to realign them, leading to a more fulfilling and purposeful career. This alignment allowed her to channel her energy and efforts towards pursuits that resonated deeply with her core values.

For fulfillment and success, goals must match values. We gain intrinsic motivation and authenticity by aligning our plans with our values. We can find happiness, purpose, and win by identifying our values and aligning our goals.

Chapter 3

Cultivating Courage

Understanding Courage

Courage is an essential virtue that enables individuals to face challenges, take risks, and overcome obstacles to pursue their goals and ideals. It is the ability to act in fear, adversity, or uncertainty, demonstrating strength, resilience, and determination. Understanding courage involves recognizing its nature, characteristics, and significance in various aspects of life. Here are key points to consider when seeking to understand courage:

1. Facing Fear: Courage involves confronting fear and acting despite it. It is not the absence of fear but the willingness to move forward despite its presence. Courageous individuals acknowledge their fears but do not allow them to paralyze or limit their actions. They push beyond their comfort zones, embracing discomfort and uncertainty as catalysts for growth.

2. Inner Strength and Resilience: Courage is rooted in inner strength and resilience. It requires mental and emotional fortitude to persevere in adversity or setbacks. Courageous individuals tap into their inner reserves of strength, determination, and self-belief to navigate challenging circumstances and emerge stronger.

3. Taking Risks: Courage often involves taking calculated risks. It means stepping into the unknown, venturing into uncharted territory, and embracing the possibility of failure. Courageous individuals understand that risk-taking is essential for personal and professional growth. They are

willing to take calculated risks, learn from the outcomes, and adapt their strategies accordingly.

4. Moral and Ethical Courage: Courage extends beyond physical acts and includes moral and ethical dimensions. Moral courage involves standing up for one's principles, speaking out against injustice, and doing what is right, even in the face of opposition. It requires integrity, conviction, and a willingness to challenge the status quo for the greater good.

5. Courageous Leadership: Courage is an essential attribute of effective leadership. Leaders who embody courage inspire and motivate others. They are willing to make tough decisions, take responsibility for their actions, and champion positive change. Courageous leaders lead by example, fostering an environment where others feel empowered to embrace their courage.

6. Growth and Personal Development: Courageous individuals embrace challenges and see them as opportunities for growth. They understand that personal development and self-discovery often occur outside their comfort zones. They expand their capabilities, knowledge, and resilience by facing fears, taking risks, and embracing new experiences.

7. Everyday Acts of Courage: Courage is not solely reserved for extraordinary circumstances but manifests in daily acts. Small acts of courage, such as speaking up, advocating for oneself, or expressing vulnerability, contribute to personal growth and foster positive change in personal and professional relationships.

8. Cultivating Courage: Courage can be developed and nurtured through intentional practice. By gradually facing

fears, setting challenging goals, and taking calculated risks, individuals can expand their comfort zones and strengthen their courage muscles. Surrounding oneself with supportive and like-minded individuals can also provide encouragement and inspiration along the journey.

In summary, courage requires understanding its nature, traits, and role. Courage helps people overcome fears, take risks, be resilient, and achieve their goals. Courage helps people overcome obstacles, grow, and help others.

Overcoming Fear and Taking Risks

Fear is a natural and spontaneous response that can keep us from reaching our full potential. However, overcoming fear and taking risks is essential for personal growth, achieving goals, and embracing new opportunities. Here are key points to consider when seeking to overcome fear and take risks:

1. Recognize the Source of Fear: Understanding the root cause of fear is the first step in overcoming it. Is the fear based on past experiences, limiting beliefs, or the fear of the unknown? By identifying the source of anxiety, you can address it directly and challenge its validity.

2. Embrace a Growth Mindset: Adopting a growth mindset is crucial when overcoming fear and taking risks. Believe in your ability to learn, adapt, and grow from experiences, even if they don't turn out as expected. See challenges as opportunities for personal development and view failure as a stepping stone toward success.

3. Set Clear Goals and Define Risks: Clearly define your goals and the potential risks. By understanding the possible consequences and weighing them against the potential

rewards, you can make informed decisions and approach risks with a balanced perspective.

4. Start with Small Steps: Small steps allow you to build confidence and overcome fear gradually. Break down more immense risks into more minor, manageable actions. Celebrate each small success, reinforcing your ability to overcome fear and take risks.

5. Prepare and Gain Knowledge: Thorough preparation and acquiring knowledge about the risks involved can alleviate fear. Research, gather information, and seek guidance from experts or mentors with experience in the area you're venturing into. The more you know, the more confident you'll take calculated risks.

6. Challenge Negative Self-Talk: Negative self-talk can amplify fear and hinder progress. Replace self-limiting beliefs with positive affirmations and constructive thoughts. Remind yourself of past successes and strengths, demonstrating your ability to overcome challenges.

7. Embrace Discomfort and Uncertainty: Taking risks inherently involves stepping outside your comfort zone and facing uncertainty. Embrace discomfort as a sign of growth and view anticipation as an opportunity for new experiences and possibilities. Remember that some of the most rewarding achievements come from pushing beyond familiar boundaries.

8. Learn from Setbacks: Setbacks and failures are part of taking risks. Instead of viewing them as defeats, see them as valuable learning experiences. Analyze what went wrong, identify lessons, and use that knowledge to adjust your approach for future endeavors.

9. Surround Yourself with Support: Seek support from individuals who believe in you and your goals. Surrounding yourself with a supportive network can provide encouragement, guidance, and reassurance when facing fears and taking risks. Their belief in you can bolster your self-confidence.

10. Celebrate Your Courage: Acknowledge and celebrate your courage in overcoming fear and taking risks. Recognize the progress you've made and the personal growth you've achieved. Regardless of the outcome, each step forward is a testament to your bravery and willingness to embrace new challenges.

By overcoming fear and taking calculated risks, you expand your comfort zone, open doors to new opportunities, and foster personal growth. Embracing these challenges allows you to discover your capabilities, build resilience, and create a life filled with meaningful experiences and accomplishments. Remember that the most significant rewards often lie just beyond the threshold of fear.

Developing Resilience

Resilience is the ability to bounce back, adapt, and recover from adversity, challenges, and setbacks. It is a crucial trait that empowers individuals to navigate life's ups and downs with strength, perseverance, and emotional well-being. Developing resilience involves cultivating certain attitudes, behaviors, and strategies that promote resilience. Here are key points to consider when seeking to build resilience:

1. Embrace a Positive Mindset: Adopting a positive mindset is foundational to building resilience. Focus on your strengths and resources rather than dwelling on limitations

or failures. Cultivate optimism, gratitude, and self-compassion to maintain a positive outlook during difficult times.

2. Cultivate Self-Care: Prioritize self-care to support your emotional, physical, and mental well-being. Engage in activities that nourish and replenish you, such as exercise, healthy eating, restful sleep, and hobbies. Taking care of yourself equips you with the energy and resilience to face challenges effectively.

3. Foster Supportive Relationships: Build and nurture relationships with supportive and understanding individuals. Surrounding yourself with a network of friends, family, mentors, or support groups can provide emotional support, encouragement, and different perspectives during challenging times.

4. Develop Problem-Solving Skills: Strengthen your problem-solving skills to navigate obstacles effectively. Break challenges into smaller, manageable tasks, and brainstorm potential solutions. Embrace a proactive approach and seek creative alternatives when faced with setbacks.

5. Practice Adaptability and Flexibility: Develop the ability to adapt and be flexible in the face of change. Embrace uncertainty as an opportunity for growth and learning. Cultivate a mindset that welcomes change and seeks new perspectives and solutions.

6. Learn from Setbacks: View setbacks and failures as valuable learning experiences. Instead of dwelling on what went wrong, focus on the lessons gained. Analyze the situation objectively, identify areas for improvement, and use that knowledge to enhance future outcomes.

7. Develop Emotional Intelligence: Enhance your emotional intelligence by effectively recognizing and managing your emotions. Build self-awareness, regulate your emotions, and cultivate empathy towards others. Emotional intelligence enables you to navigate challenges with resilience and maintain healthy relationships.

8. Set Realistic Goals: Set realistic and achievable goals to maintain motivation and a sense of progress. Break larger goals into smaller milestones, celebrating achievements along the way. This approach allows you to maintain focus, build momentum, and experience a sense of accomplishment.

9. Practice Self-Reflection: Regularly self-reflect to gain insight into your thoughts, emotions, and reactions. Understand how you respond to adversity and identify patterns or behaviors that may hinder resilience. Self-reflection promotes self-awareness and helps you develop strategies to overcome challenges effectively.

10. Cultivate Optimism and Gratitude: Foster optimism and gratitude by focusing on the positive aspects of your life. Practice gratitude daily by acknowledging and appreciating the blessings, achievements, and supportive relationships. Optimism and gratitude enhance resilience by fostering a positive outlook and reducing stress.

By consciously developing resilience, you equip yourself with the tools and mindset to navigate life's challenges more effectively. Resilience empowers you to bounce back from setbacks, adapt to change, and maintain well-being during difficult times. Remember that resilience is a skill that can be nurtured and strengthened through practice and self-reflection, enabling you to face adversity with greater strength and fortitude.

Chapter 4

The Power of Focus

Concentration and Mental Clarity

Concentration and mental clarity are essential cognitive abilities contributing to productivity, effective decision-making, and overall well-being. They involve the ability to focus one's attention, block out distractions, and maintain a clear and sharp mental state. Here are key points to consider when exploring concentration and mental clarity:

1. Focus and Attention: Concentration is directing and sustaining focused attention on a specific task or object. It involves immersing oneself in the present moment and minimizing distractions. Developing the skill of concentration allows for enhanced productivity and efficiency in completing tasks.

2. Mindfulness Practice: Mindfulness is a powerful technique for cultivating concentration and mental clarity. By practicing mindfulness, individuals learn to observe their thoughts and emotions without judgment, thereby reducing mental clutter and enhancing the transparency of the mind. Mindfulness meditation exercises can strengthen the brain's ability to sustain attention and improve overall mental focus.

3. Prioritization and Time Management: Effectively managing one's time and prioritizing tasks can support concentration and mental clarity. Breaking down larger tasks into smaller, manageable segments and setting clear priorities can help reduce overwhelm and improve focus on the task at hand.

4. Physical Well-being: Physical well-being directly affects mental clarity and concentration. Regular physical exercise, a balanced diet, and enough sleep are crucial for optimizing brain function. Physical activity boosts circulation, oxygenates the brain, and enhances cognitive abilities.

5. Minimize Distractions: Creating an environment conducive to concentration is essential. Minimize external distractions, such as noise, clutter, and interruptions, to promote mental clarity. Use techniques like setting boundaries, utilizing noise-canceling headphones, or finding a quiet space when concentration is required.

6. Mental Breaks and Rest: Regular breaks and incorporating rest periods into one's routine can enhance concentration and mental clarity. Fatigue and mental exhaustion can impede focus and diminish cognitive abilities. Engaging in activities like walking, deep breathing, or practicing relaxation techniques can rejuvenate the mind and improve mental clarity.

7. Clearing Mental Clutter: Mental clarity is achieved by decluttering the mind of excessive thoughts, worries, and distractions. Journaling, practicing gratitude, or engaging in reflective exercises can help declutter the mind and create mental space for improved concentration.

8. Limiting Multitasking: Multitasking can be counterproductive regarding concentration and mental clarity. While it may seem efficient, constantly switching between tasks can reduce focus and increase mental strain. Prioritize tasks and engage in one study at a time to maintain mental clarity and improve productivity.

9. Cognitive Enhancement Techniques: Various techniques can enhance cognitive abilities and promote mental clarity.

These include brain-training exercises, puzzles, reading, and engaging in activities that challenge and stimulate the mind. These activities help sharpen mental acuity and improve concentration.

10. Healthy Mindset and Self-Care: Cultivating a positive and healthy mindset supports concentration and mental clarity. Practicing self-care, engaging in activities that bring joy and relaxation, and maintaining healthy boundaries contribute to overall well-being and cognitive function.

Individuals can optimize their cognitive abilities and improve their overall performance and well-being by cultivating concentration and mental clarity. These abilities allow for better focus, productivity, and decision-making, leading to tremendous success and a more fulfilling life. Embracing practices that support concentration and mental clarity can contribute to a clear and focused mind, fostering personal and professional growth.

Eliminating Distractions

In our fast-paced and technology-driven world, distractions can hinder productivity, focus, and overall performance. Eliminating distractions is crucial for maintaining concentration, enhancing efficiency, and achieving goals. Here are key points to consider when seeking to eliminate distractions:

1. Identify Common Distractions: Identify the specific distractions that commonly disrupt your focus. These can include notifications on your phone, social media, email alerts, environmental noise, or even internal distractions like wandering thoughts. Understanding your typical sources of distraction is the first step in addressing them effectively.

2. Create a Distraction-Free Environment: Designate a physical workspace that minimizes external distractions. Find a quiet area, organize your desk, and remove unnecessary clutter. Consider using noise-canceling headphones or a "Do Not Disturb" sign to signal to others that you are in a focused mode.

3. Digital Detox: Technology can be a significant source of distraction. Temporarily disconnect from social media platforms, mute notifications on your devices, and use apps or browser extensions that block access to time-wasting websites. Set boundaries around the technology used to create a more focused, distraction-free environment.

4. Establish Clear Boundaries: Communicate your need for uninterrupted work time to colleagues, family members, or roommates. Establish specific periods during the day when you are not to be disturbed unless it's an emergency. Setting boundaries helps others understand and respect your need for concentration.

5. Prioritize and Time Block: Prioritize your tasks and allocate specific time blocks for focused work. Use time management techniques like the Pomodoro Technique, where you work in concentrated bursts followed by short breaks. Dedicating particular time slots to different activities can reduce the temptation to multitask and increase productivity.

6. Practice Mindfulness and Meditation: Incorporate mindfulness and meditation practices into your routine. These techniques train your mind to stay present, observe distractions without engaging with them, and redirect your attention to the task. Regular mindfulness practice can

improve your ability to resist distractions and maintain focus.

7. Create a Task-Driven Environment: Establish a clear plan for each work session. Break down larger tasks into smaller, actionable steps. A structured program helps you stay on track and reduces the likelihood of getting sidetracked by distractions.

8. Seek Accountability: Find an accountability partner or join a productivity group where you can share your goals and progress. Being held accountable by others can motivate you to stay focused and eliminate distractions.

Case Study:

As a marketing professional, Sarah struggled with distractions that hindered her productivity and focus. She constantly checked her phone for notifications, responded to emails as soon as they arrived, and got sidetracked by social media. As a result, she often missed deadlines and felt overwhelmed by her workload.

Sarah decided to eliminate distractions and create a more focused work environment to address this issue. She turned off non-essential notifications on her phone and established specific times to check and respond to emails. She installed a website blocker on her browser to prevent access to social media during work hours. Sarah also designated a dedicated workspace at home and informed her family about her need for uninterrupted time.

Additionally, Sarah started using time-blocking techniques, allocating specific periods for focused work and scheduling breaks in between. She practiced mindfulness meditation for a few minutes daily to train her mind to stay present and resist distractions. Sarah also joined a productivity group where she shared her goals and progress, receiving support and accountability from like-minded individuals.

By implementing these strategies, Sarah experienced a significant improvement in her focus and productivity. She completed tasks more efficiently, met deadlines, and felt less overwhelmed by distractions. Eliminating distractions allowed her to fully engage in her work, resulting in better quality output and increased satisfaction in her professional life.

Eliminating distractions requires discipline and conscious effort, but the benefits are worth it. Creating a focused environment and implementing strategies to minimize interruptions can optimize productivity, enhance concentration, and achieve tremendous success.

Practicing Mindfulness

Mindfulness is fully present and engaged in the present moment, with a non-judgmental and accepting attitude. It involves directing attention to our thoughts, feelings, bodily sensations, and the environment without getting caught up in judgments or distractions. Here are key points to consider when exploring mindfulness:

1. Cultivating Awareness: Mindfulness enables a heightened sense of self-awareness. By paying attention to our thoughts, emotions, and physical sensations, we develop a deeper understanding of ourselves and our inner experiences. This awareness allows us to respond to situations with clarity and intention rather than reacting automatically.

2. Living in the Present: Mindfulness emphasizes the importance of focusing on the present moment. It

encourages us to let go of dwelling on the past or worrying about the future and instead fully engage in what is happening right now. Being present allows us to savor experiences, improve our concentration, and reduce stress.

3. Non-Judgmental Attitude: Mindfulness involves adopting a non-judgmental and accepting attitude toward our experiences. Rather than labeling our thoughts or emotions as good or bad, we observe them with curiosity and without judgment. This practice helps reduce self-criticism and fosters self-compassion.

4. Managing Stress and Emotions: Mindfulness can be a powerful tool for managing stress and regulating emotions. By observing our thoughts and feelings without getting swept away, we can respond more calmly and clearly to challenging situations. Mindfulness techniques, such as deep breathing or body scans, can help us ground ourselves and find balance amidst stress.

5. Enhancing Focus and Concentration: Regular mindfulness practice strengthens our ability to sustain attention and improves our focus. By training our minds to stay present and redirect our attention when it wanders, we become more effective at tasks, enhance productivity, and reduce mental distractions.

6. Cultivating Gratitude and Happiness: Mindfulness encourages us to appreciate and savor life's simple pleasures. By directing our attention to the positive aspects of our experiences and producing gratitude, we can enhance our overall well-being and happiness.

7. Building Resilience: Mindfulness can contribute to building emotional resilience. By developing the ability to observe and accept our thoughts and emotions, we become

better equipped to navigate challenging situations and bounce back from setbacks.

8. Mindful Relationships: Practicing mindfulness can also improve our relationships. By being fully present and attentive when interacting, we cultivate deeper connections and foster effective communication.

9. Incorporating Daily Mindfulness: Mindfulness can be practiced formally through activities like meditation or yoga and informally in our daily lives. Engaging in simple practices such as mindful eating, mindful walking, or taking mindful pauses throughout the day can help us integrate mindfulness into our routines.

10. Continuous Practice: Mindfulness is a skill that develops over time with consistent practice. Like any other skill, it requires dedication and patience. Regular training, even for just a few minutes daily, can profoundly affect our well-being and overall quality of life.

By embracing mindfulness, we can bring greater awareness, peace, and clarity to our lives. It enables us to be more fully present, reduce stress, enhance our relationships, and cultivate a greater sense of overall well-being. Mindfulness allows us to slow down, connect with ourselves and the world around us, and live with greater intention and joy.

Chapter 5

Developing Habits and Routines

Creating Positive Habits

Habits play a significant role in shaping our lives and determining our success. Positive habits are essential for personal growth, productivity, and overall well-being. Here are key points to consider when seeking to create positive habits:

1. Identify the Desired Habits: Identify the specific habits you want to develop. Consider areas of your life where positive changes would have the most significant impact. Whether exercising regularly, practicing gratitude, or creating a reading habit, clearly define the patterns you wish to cultivate.

2. Start Small: Start with small, achievable steps to build momentum and increase the likelihood of success. Break down the habit into minor actions that are easy to incorporate into your daily routine. Starting small reduces overwhelm and makes it easier to maintain consistency.

3. Set Clear Goals: Set clear and specific goals for each habit you want to develop. Define what success looks like and establish measurable targets. Having specific goals creates a sense of direction and clearly focuses your efforts.

4. Create a Routine: Establish a routine that supports the development of your desired habits. Consistency is key in habit formation. Schedule specific times or triggers that remind you to engage in the desired behavior throughout your day. Over time, the habit will become more automatic and integrated into your daily life.

5. Track Your Progress: Keep track of your progress to stay motivated and accountable. Use tools like habit trackers, journals, or apps to monitor your daily actions and measure your progress. Seeing your progress visually can provide a sense of accomplishment and reinforce positive habits.

6. Stay Committed and Persistent: Building new habits takes time and effort. Stay committed to your goals and be persistent, even if you face setbacks or challenges. Remind yourself of the benefits and the long-term impact of cultivating positive habits.

7. Surround Yourself with Support: Seek support from like-minded individuals who share your goals or have successfully developed similar habits. Join groups, find an accountability partner, or seek mentorship to provide encouragement, guidance, and motivation on your habit-building journey.

8. Focus on Self-Care: Prioritize self-care to ensure your physical and mental well-being. Habits are more easily developed when you are taking care of yourself. Get enough sleep, eat nourishing foods, exercise regularly, and manage stress effectively. Taking care of yourself provides the foundation for developing positive habits.

9. Celebrate Milestones: Celebrate your achievements and milestones along the way. Recognize and reward yourself for maintaining consistency and making progress. Celebrating small victories reinforces positive habits and strengthens your motivation to continue.

10. Embrace a Growth Mindset: Adopt a growth mindset recognizing that habits can be developed and changed over time. Embrace the belief that you can create positive habits

and that setbacks or failures are opportunities for learning and growth.

By consciously creating positive habits, you can transform your life and achieve personal and professional success. You can develop habits that align with your values and goals through consistent practice, dedication, and a supportive mindset, leading to long-lasting positive change and fulfilling life.

Breaking Bad Habits

Bad habits can hinder personal growth, productivity, and overall well-being. Breaking these habits is crucial for making positive changes and achieving our goals. Here are key points to consider when seeking to break bad habits:

1. Identify the Habit: Identify the bad habit you want to break. Clearly define the behavior or routine that you want to eliminate from your life. This self-awareness is the first step in initiating change.

2. Understand the Triggers: Explore the triggers or cues that lead to the bad habit. Triggers can be environmental, emotional, or situational factors that prompt the practice. You can develop strategies to avoid or manage the behavior by understanding what triggers the behavior.

3. Replace with Positive Alternatives: Instead of simply eliminating a bad habit, focus on replacing it with a positive alternative. Identify healthier behaviors or routines that can fulfill the same need or desire. This helps redirect your energy and provides a positive outlet for the habit.

4. Set Clear Goals and Action Plans: Set clear goals for breaking bad habits and specific action plans. Define

measurable targets and create a step-by-step plan to gradually reduce or eliminate the practice. Break down the process into smaller, achievable tasks to maintain motivation and track progress.

5. Create Accountability: Hold yourself accountable for breaking the bad habit. Share your goals with trusted friends or family members who can support and hold you responsible. Consider joining support groups or seeking professional help if needed. Accountability helps maintain motivation and guides during challenging times.

6. Modify the Environment: Modify your environment to make it less conducive to bad habits. Remove triggers or cues that prompt the behavior. Rearrange your physical space, create barriers, or introduce new alerts that support positive habits.

7. Practice Self-Reflection: Regularly self-reflect to understand the underlying reasons behind the bad habit. Identify any emotional or psychological factors that contribute to the behavior. This self-awareness helps address the root causes and develop strategies for long-term change.

8. Implement Replacement Strategies: Develop specific strategies to cope with the urges or cravings associated with the bad habit. Find healthier ways to deal with stress, boredom, or other triggers. For example, if you're trying to quit smoking, you could replace it with deep breathing exercises or chewing sugar-free gum.

9. Consistency and Persistence: Breaking bad habits requires consistency and persistence. Be patient with yourself and acknowledge that change takes time. Stay committed to your goals even if you experience setbacks or relapses.

Learn from those moments and use them as opportunities for growth.

10. Celebrate Progress: Celebrate your progress along the way. Recognize and reward yourself for every milestone and accomplishment. Celebrating small victories boosts motivation and reinforces the positive changes you're making.

Case Study:

John had a habit of procrastinating, which greatly affected his productivity and caused unnecessary stress. He often postponed essential tasks until the last minute, resulting in rushed work and missed deadlines. To break this habit, John implemented the following strategies:

1. He identified the triggers of his procrastination, such as feeling overwhelmed by the size of a task or being easily distracted by social media.

2. John set clear goals and created an action plan. He broke down his tasks into smaller, manageable steps and set deadlines for each step. This helped him stay focused and motivated.

3. He created accountability by sharing his goals with a trusted friend who regularly checks his progress. This helped him stay committed and motivated to overcome his habit of procrastination.

4. John modified his environment by using website blockers to limit access to distracting websites and creating a designated workspace free from distractions.

5. He practiced self-reflection and identified that fear of failure was one of the underlying reasons for his

procrastination. He worked on developing a growth mindset and reframing failure as an opportunity for learning and growth.

6. John implemented replacement strategies to deal with his urges to procrastinate. He used techniques like the Pomodoro Technique, where he worked in focused intervals followed by short breaks and practiced visualization exercises to imagine the sense of accomplishment and relief, he would feel by completing tasks on time.

Over time, John successfully broke his habit of procrastination. By implementing these strategies and staying consistent, he improved his productivity, reduced stress, and achieved better results in his work. Breaking the bad habit of procrastination made him more efficient, organized, and successful personally and professionally.

Breaking bad habits requires commitment, self-discipline, and a willingness to change. By implementing targeted strategies and staying persistent, individuals can break free from negative patterns and create a more positive and fulfilling life.

Establishing Effective Daily Routines

Daily routines provide structure, efficiency, and productivity to our lives. They help us prioritize tasks, manage time effectively, and maintain balance and well-being. Here are key points to consider when establishing effective daily routines:

1. Set Clear Goals: Start by defining your goals and priorities. Determine what you want to accomplish each day and what areas require attention. Clear goals provide a sense of direction and purpose.

2. Identify Essential Tasks: Identify the essential tasks for your daily routine. These tasks include work-related responsibilities, personal care, exercise, family time, and self-care activities. Prioritize the most critical tasks to ensure they are completed.

3. Create a Schedule: Establish a schedule that outlines the timing and sequence of your daily activities. Allocate specific time slots for different tasks, allowing for flexibility and breaks. Structure your day to optimize your energy levels and maximize productivity.

4. Morning Rituals: Start your day with a morning routine that sets a positive tone for the rest of the day. Include activities such as meditation, exercise, journaling, or reading. This helps create a sense of focus, clarity, and mental preparedness.

5. Time Blocking: Utilize time-blocking techniques to allocate dedicated time slots for specific activities. Assign blocks of time for focused work, meetings, breaks, and personal activities. This helps minimize distractions and increases productivity.

6. Prioritize Important Tasks: Identify the most critical and high-priority tasks, and tackle them during peak energy periods. This ensures crucial work is completed when you are at your best and most focused.

7. Build in Breaks and Rest: Incorporate regular breaks into your daily routine. Breaks help recharge your energy, reduce stress, and improve overall productivity. Schedule short breaks for stretching, walking, or relaxing to avoid burnout.

8. Flexibility and Adaptability: Allow flexibility in your routine to accommodate unexpected events or changing priorities. Be open to adjusting your schedule when necessary while maintaining a sense of structure and discipline.

9. Review and Reflect: At the end of each day, review your accomplishments, evaluate your progress, and plan for the next day. Reflecting on your daily routines helps identify areas for improvement and ensures continuous growth.

10. Self-Care and Mindfulness: Prioritize self-care activities such as adequate sleep, healthy eating, and relaxation techniques. Incorporate moments of mindfulness throughout the day to stay present and reduce stress.

Establishing effective daily routines helps optimize productivity, improve time management, and enhance overall well-being. By setting clear goals, creating structured schedules, and incorporating self-care activities, individuals can make a balanced and fulfilling daily routine that supports their goals and priorities.

Chapter 6

Emotional Intelligence and Self-Control

Understanding Emotional Intelligence

Emotional intelligence refers to the ability to recognize, understand, and manage our own emotions as well as the emotions of others. It involves being aware of our feelings, having empathy for others, and effectively regulating emotions in different situations. Here are key points to consider when understanding emotional intelligence:

1. Self-Awareness: Emotional intelligence begins with self-awareness. It involves recognizing and understanding our emotions, strengths, weaknesses, and triggers. By being aware of our emotional state, we can better manage our reactions and make more conscious decisions.

2. Self-Regulation: Emotional intelligence includes the ability to regulate and control our emotions. It involves managing impulsive behaviors, responding appropriately to different situations, and adapting to changing circumstances. Self-regulation helps prevent emotional outbursts and promotes calm and thoughtful responses.

3. Empathy: Empathy is the ability to understand and share the feelings of others. Emotional intelligence enables us to put ourselves in someone else's shoes, recognize their emotions, and respond sensitively. Empathy fosters better communication, stronger relationships, and a sense of connectedness with others.

4. Social Skills: Emotional intelligence encompasses practical social skills. It involves navigating social interactions,

building and maintaining relationships, and communicating effectively. Good social skills enable collaboration, conflict resolution, and cooperation with others.

5. Recognizing Emotions in Others: Emotional intelligence allows us to recognize and understand the emotions of others. It involves picking up on verbal and nonverbal cues, such as facial expressions, body language, and tone of voice. This understanding helps us respond appropriately and support others emotionally.

6. Emotional Resilience: Emotional intelligence contributes to emotional resilience, which is the ability to bounce back from setbacks and cope with adversity. It involves recognizing and managing negative emotions, seeking support when needed, and maintaining a positive outlook in challenging situations.

7. Conflict Management: Emotional intelligence helps in managing conflicts constructively. It involves understanding differing perspectives, empathizing with others' emotions, and finding win-win solutions. Emotional intelligence promotes healthier relationships and a positive work or personal environment by managing conflicts effectively.

8. Decision Making: Emotional intelligence plays a role in decision-making processes. It involves considering both rational thinking and emotional factors when making choices. By incorporating emotional intelligence, we can make more balanced and well-informed decisions.

9. Continuous Development: Emotional intelligence can be developed and improved over time. It requires self-reflection, self-awareness, and a willingness to learn and

grow. Engaging in mindfulness, self-assessment, and seeking feedback can enhance emotional intelligence.

10. Personal and Professional Benefits: Emotional intelligence has numerous personal and professional benefits. It improves communication skills, enhances leadership abilities, fosters teamwork, and promotes well-being and satisfaction in personal relationships and work environments.

Understanding emotional intelligence allows individuals to navigate their own emotions and the emotions of others with greater awareness and skill. Individuals can build stronger relationships, manage conflicts effectively, make better decisions, and lead a more fulfilling and successful life by cultivating emotional intelligence.

Managing Emotions

Managing emotions is recognizing, understanding, and regulating our emotions in various situations. It involves effectively handling both positive and negative emotions to maintain emotional balance and make informed decisions. Here are key points to consider when it comes to managing emotions:

1. Emotional Awareness: Managing emotions starts with being aware of our emotional states. It involves recognizing and acknowledging the feelings we are experiencing at any given moment. Developing emotional awareness allows us to understand the underlying reasons for our emotions and how they impact our thoughts and behaviors.

2. Emotion Regulation: Emotion regulation involves managing and controlling our emotions appropriately. It includes strategies such as deep breathing, mindfulness,

and reframing negative thoughts. Emotion regulation helps prevent impulsive reactions and allows for more thoughtful responses in challenging situations.

3. Self-Care: Taking care of ourselves physically, mentally, and emotionally is vital for managing emotions. Engaging in activities that promote relaxation, such as exercise, meditation, or hobbies, helps reduce stress and enhances emotional well-being. Prioritizing self-care enables us to better handle and cope with emotions.

4. Stress Management: Effective stress management is crucial for managing emotions. Stress can intensify emotions and lead to adverse outcomes. Implementing stress management techniques like exercise, time management, and seeking social support helps alleviate stress and promotes emotional resilience.

5. Developing Empathy: Empathy plays a significant role in managing emotions in ourselves and our interactions with others. Developing empathy allows us to understand and validate the feelings of others, enhancing our communication and fostering healthier relationships.

6. Seeking Support: When emotions become overwhelming, seeking support from trusted individuals can be helpful. Sharing our feelings and concerns with others provides a sense of relief and allows for perspective and guidance. Help from friends, family, or professionals can assist in managing emotions more effectively.

7. Positive Coping Strategies: Developing positive coping strategies helps manage emotions healthily. Engaging in activities that bring joy, practicing relaxation techniques, journaling, or seeking professional help are examples of positive coping strategies. These strategies allow for the

expression and processing of emotions in constructive ways.

8. Reflection and Learning: Reflecting on and learning from past emotional experiences improves dynamic management. Identifying patterns, triggers, and the impact of emotions on our behavior helps develop effective strategies for managing emotions in the future.

9. Emotional Intelligence: Building emotional intelligence is closely tied to managing emotions. Developing self-awareness, empathy, and self-regulation skills improves our ability to understand and manage emotions effectively in ourselves and others.

10. Practice and Patience: Managing emotions is an ongoing process that requires practice and patience. Understanding that developing the skills necessary for managing emotions effectively takes time is essential. We can improve our emotional management over time with consistent effort and a growth mindset.

By actively managing our emotions, we can navigate life's challenges more effectively, make better decisions, and cultivate healthier relationships. Learning to recognize, understand, and regulate our feelings empowers us to respond in ways that align with our values and goals, leading to greater emotional well-being and overall life satisfaction.

Developing Self-Control

Self-control regulates our thoughts, emotions, and behaviors to achieve long-term goals and make rational decisions. It involves managing impulses, delaying gratification, and staying focused on what truly matters. Here are key points to consider when developing self-control:

1. Awareness: Developing self-control starts with understanding our thoughts, emotions, and behaviors. Recognize situations or triggers that lead to impulsive or undesirable actions. Self-awareness allows us to pause and assess our responses before acting on them.

2. Goal Setting: Set clear and meaningful goals that align with your values and aspirations. Having well-defined goals helps provide motivation and acts as a compass for decision-making. Set both short-term and long-term goals to keep yourself focused and disciplined.

3. Emotional Regulation: Emotions can often drive impulsive actions. Learn to regulate your emotions by identifying and understanding them. Practice deep breathing, mindfulness, or calming techniques to manage emotional responses and prevent impulsive behavior.

4. Developing Willpower: Willpower is the mental strength to resist short-term temptations for long-term benefits. Build your willpower by gradually exposing yourself to situations that challenge your self-control. Start with small changes and progressively increase the difficulty to strengthen your self-discipline.

5. Delayed Gratification: Delayed gratification involves resisting immediate desires for greater rewards in the future. Train yourself to resist impulsive urges and focus

on the long-term benefits of delayed gratification. This helps build resilience and patience.

6. Establish Routines: Create structured routines and habits that support your goals and promote self-control. Consistent and disciplined performances reduce the need for constant decision-making and preserve mental energy for more critical tasks.

7. Accountability and Support: Seek accountability by sharing your goals and progress with trusted individuals. Having someone to hold you accountable can help maintain your commitment to self-control. Additionally, seek support from friends, mentors, or support groups who can provide guidance and encouragement during challenging times.

8. Stress Management: High levels of stress can diminish self-control. Develop effective stress management techniques such as exercise, relaxation, and self-care to minimize stress levels. When pressure is reduced, it becomes easier to maintain self-control.

9. Practice Mindfulness: Cultivate mindfulness to stay present and aware of your thoughts, emotions, and actions. Mindfulness helps you observe your impulses and allows you to make conscious choices instead of reacting impulsively.

10. Learn from Setbacks: Embrace setbacks and learn from them. Mistakes and failures are opportunities for growth and improvement. Reflect on what went wrong, identify areas for improvement, and adjust your approach accordingly.

Developing self-control requires patience, practice, and self-reflection. By consciously improving self-control, individuals can make more deliberate choices, resist temptations, and achieve long-term success and personal growth. Self-control becomes a valuable skill that enhances various aspects of life with consistent effort.

Chapter 7

Perseverance and Grit

The Role of Perseverance in Success

Perseverance is steadfastness and persistence in pursuing goals, despite challenges, setbacks, or obstacles. It plays a crucial role in achieving success and reaching one's full potential. Here are key points to consider regarding the part of perseverance in victory:

1. Overcoming Challenges: Perseverance enables individuals to face and overcome challenges that arise on their path to success. It fosters resilience, determination, and overcoming difficulties without giving up.

2. Resilience: Perseverance builds strength, which is the ability to bounce back from failures and setbacks. It helps individuals maintain a positive mindset, learn from failures, and progress despite obstacles or disappointments.

3. Goal Achievement: Perseverance is essential for reaching long-term goals. Success often requires sustained effort, commitment, and the willingness to persevere even when progress is slow or uncertain. It ensures that individuals stay focused and dedicated to their objectives.

4. Learning and Growth: Perseverance encourages a growth mindset, where setbacks and failures are viewed as opportunities for learning and growth. It promotes continuous improvement and the willingness to adapt and adjust strategies to achieve success.

5. Building Character and Discipline: Perseverance develops character traits such as discipline, patience, and

determination. It instills a strong work ethic and commitment to tasks, even when motivation wanes.

6. Overcoming Fear and Doubt: Perseverance helps individuals overcome fear, self-doubt, and uncertainty. It allows them to push beyond their comfort zones, take risks, and embrace new opportunities, ultimately leading to personal and professional growth.

7. Building Momentum: Perseverance creates momentum. Individuals build momentum that propels them forward by consistently putting in effort and taking small steps toward their goals. This momentum becomes a driving force in achieving success.

8. Inspiring Others: Perseverance serves as a source of inspiration for others. When individuals demonstrate unwavering dedication and perseverance, they encourage those around them to pursue their goals and dreams with determination.

9. Achieving Extraordinary Results: Many achievements and breakthroughs would not be possible without perseverance. History is filled with stories of individuals who faced countless failures and rejections but persevered, ultimately achieving extraordinary success.

10. Personal Fulfillment: Perseverance brings a sense of personal fulfillment and satisfaction. Staying towards goals and overcoming challenges builds character, resilience, and a deep understanding of accomplishment.

Perseverance is a fundamental quality that distinguishes those who achieve success from those who give up. It is the driving force behind progress, growth, and realizing one's full potential. By embracing perseverance, individuals can overcome obstacles, achieve their goals, and create a meaningful and successful life.

Cultivating Grit

Grit combines passion, perseverance, and resilience in pursuing long-term goals. It is the ability to stay committed and resilient in facing challenges, setbacks, and adversity. Cultivating grit is essential for achieving success and personal growth. Here are key points to consider when it comes to developing spirit:

1. Passion and Purpose: Grit begins with having a strong sense of warmth and purpose. Identifying and pursuing goals that align with your values and ignite your enthusiasm fuels the determination and perseverance required to overcome obstacles.

2. Perseverance: Grit entails a steadfast commitment to working hard and persisting through difficulties. It involves staying focused on the long-term objective and not being deterred by short-term setbacks or failures.

3. Resilience: Resilience is a core component of grit. It is the ability to bounce back from adversity, learn from failures, and keep moving forward. Developing resilience helps individuals adapt to challenges and setbacks, emerging more substantial and more determined.

4. Growth Mindset: Cultivating a growth mindset is crucial for grit. Embracing the belief that abilities and skills can be developed through effort and learning enables individuals to view challenges as opportunities for growth rather than insurmountable obstacles.

5. Embracing Discomfort: Grit requires stepping out of one's comfort zone and embracing discomfort. It involves taking calculated risks, facing fears, and seeking challenges that foster personal and professional growth.

6. Self-Discipline: Grit relies on self-discipline, the ability to prioritize, and make choices that align with long-term goals. It involves creating habits and routines that support progress, staying focused, and avoiding distractions.

7. Seeking Feedback and Learning: Gritty individuals actively seek feedback and embrace a continuous learning mindset. They view feedback as an opportunity to improve and refine their skills, making necessary adjustments to their approach.

8. Support Networks: Building strong support networks is essential for cultivating grit. Surrounding yourself with like-minded individuals with similar goals and values provides encouragement, accountability, and a sense of community.

9. Optimism and Positive Thinking: Maintaining an optimistic outlook and cultivating positive thinking contribute to grit. Seeing challenges as opportunities for growth and maintaining a positive attitude during setbacks helps individuals persevere and keep their motivation.

10. Celebrating Progress: Recognizing and celebrating small milestones and progress along the way reinforces grit. Acknowledging achievements, no matter how small, boosts motivation and confidence, fueling continued perseverance.

Cultivating grit requires dedication, determination, and a growth mindset. By embracing passion, perseverance, resilience, and a commitment to personal growth, individuals can facilitate spirit and enhance their ability to overcome challenges, achieve long-term goals, and lead a more fulfilling and successful life.

Overcoming Obstacles and Challenges

Life is filled with obstacles and challenges that can hinder our progress and success. However, overcoming these obstacles is crucial for personal growth and achieving our goals. Here are key points to consider when it comes to overcoming obstacles and challenges:

1. Positive Mindset: Adopting a positive mindset is essential when facing obstacles. Instead of viewing challenges as insurmountable roadblocks, see them as opportunities for growth and learning. Embrace a belief that you can overcome barriers and find solutions.

2. Problem-Solving: Approach obstacles with a problem-solving mindset. Break down the challenge into smaller, manageable tasks. Analyze the situation, explore different strategies, and consider alternative approaches. Engage in creative thinking to find innovative solutions.

3. Resilience: Develop resilience, the ability to bounce back from setbacks and adversity. Resilient individuals see failures as learning experiences and use them as stepping stones toward success. Cultivate the mindset that setbacks are temporary and use them as motivation to keep pushing forward.

4. Perseverance: Perseverance is crucial when facing obstacles. It involves staying committed and determined despite difficulties or setbacks. Focus on your long-term goals and

keep pushing forward, even when progress seems slow or challenging.

5. Support Systems: Seek support from others who can guide, encourage, and advise during challenging times. Surround yourself with a network of friends, mentors, or professionals who can offer support and perspective.

6. Adaptability: Be open to change and adapt your strategies when facing obstacles. Sometimes, a different approach or perspective is needed to overcome challenges. Embrace flexibility and adjust your plans accordingly.

7. Self-Reflection: Take time for self-reflection to understand your strengths, weaknesses, and areas for improvement. Reflect on past experiences and learn from them. Identify patterns or behaviors that may contribute to your obstacles and make necessary adjustments.

8. Break it Down: When facing a large or complex obstacle, break it down into smaller, more manageable tasks. Focus on one step at a time and celebrate each small victory. This approach helps maintain motivation and momentum.

9. Learn from Others: Seek inspiration from individuals who have overcome similar challenges or succeeded in your desired area. Learn from their experiences, strategies, and mindset. Their stories can provide valuable insights and guidance.

10. Self-Belief: Develop a strong belief in yourself and your abilities. Trust in your capacity to overcome obstacles and achieve your goals. Cultivate self-confidence and affirmations that reinforce your confidence in your potential.

Overcoming obstacles and challenges is an inherent part of personal and professional growth. By adopting a positive mindset, utilizing problem-solving skills, nurturing resilience, and seeking support, individuals can navigate obstacles and emerge stronger, wiser, and more capable of achieving their desired outcomes. Embrace challenges as opportunities for growth, and let them fuel your determination to succeed.

Chapter 8

Discipline in Action: Strategies and Techniques

Time Management and Prioritization

Effective time management and prioritization are essential for maximizing productivity, achieving goals, and maintaining a healthy work-life balance. Here are key points to consider when it comes to time management and prioritization:

1. Set Clear Goals: Start by setting clear and specific goals. Understand what you want to accomplish in your life, such as career, personal development, relationships, and health. Clear goals provide direction and help you prioritize your time effectively.

2. Prioritize Tasks: Prioritize tasks based on their importance and urgency. Use techniques like the Eisenhower Matrix, which categorizes tasks into four quadrants: urgent and important, important but not urgent, urgent but not essential, and neither urgent nor important. Focus your energy on studies in the acute and integral quadrants.

3. Plan Ahead: Create a daily, weekly, and monthly schedule to plan your activities. Allocate specific time slots for tasks and activities, including work, personal commitments, relaxation, and self-care. Plan your day to minimize time wasted on decision-making.

4. Avoid Procrastination: Procrastination can be a major time-waster. Recognize when you are procrastinating and identify the underlying reasons. Break tasks into smaller, manageable chunks, set deadlines, and use techniques like

the Pomodoro Technique to work in focused bursts with short breaks.

5. Delegate and Outsource: Recognize tasks that can be delegated or outsourced to others. Identify areas where you can leverage the skills and strengths of others, whether it's at work or in personal tasks. Delegating frees up your time to focus on higher-priority responsibilities.

6. Eliminate Time Wasters: Identify and eliminate activities that consume your time without adding value. Examples include excessive social media use, unproductive meetings, or engaging in tasks that could be automated or streamlined. Be mindful of how you spend your time and make adjustments accordingly.

7. Learn to Say No: Prioritize your commitments and say no to tasks or requests that don't align with your goals or priorities. Understand that your time and energy are limited resources, and it's essential to protect them by focusing on what truly matters.

8. Focus and Avoid Multitasking: Multitasking can reduce efficiency and lead to errors. Instead, practice single-tasking by dedicating your full attention to one task. Set aside distractions and create an environment that supports focus and concentration.

9. Take Breaks and Rest: Recognize the importance of breaks and rest in maintaining productivity and overall well-being. Schedule regular intervals to recharge and rejuvenate. Prioritize self-care activities, such as exercise, meditation, or hobbies, which help reduce stress and enhance focus.

10. Regularly Review and Adjust: Review your schedule, tasks, and priorities to ensure they align with your goals and values. Be flexible and willing to adjust your plans as circumstances change. Learn from your experiences and make improvements to optimize your time management strategies.

Effective time management and prioritization enable individuals to maximize their available time, reduce stress, and achieve a better work-life balance. By setting clear goals, prioritizing tasks, planning, eliminating time wasters, and taking care of yourself, you can enhance your productivity and accomplish your goals more efficiently.

Creating Accountability Structures

Creating accountability structures is essential for personal and professional growth, as it helps individuals stay focused, motivated, and committed to their goals. Accountability structures provide support, guidance, and a sense of responsibility for taking action and following through on commitments. Here are key points to consider when it comes to creating accountability structures:

1. Identify Goals and Commitments: Identify your goals and the required actions or tasks. Clearly define what you want to accomplish and set measurable objectives. Write them down to make them more tangible and concrete.

2. Find an Accountability Partner: Seek a partner who can support and hold you accountable for your actions. This can be a friend, colleague, mentor, or coach who shares similar goals or has expertise in the area you're working on. Regularly communicate with your accountability partner to update them on your progress and challenges.

3. Set Regular Check-Ins: Establish a schedule for regular check-ins with your accountability partner. This can be weekly, biweekly, or monthly, depending on the nature of your goals and the level of support you need. During these check-ins, review your progress, discuss any obstacles or setbacks, and brainstorm strategies for improvement.

4. Clearly Define Expectations: Clearly define expectations and responsibilities with your accountability partner. Discuss what kind of feedback, support, or guidance you seek and how they can best assist you. Please make sure both parties have a clear understanding of their roles in the accountability structure.

5. Use Tools and Systems: Utilize tools and systems to track your progress and hold yourself accountable. This can include using productivity apps, project management software, or goal-tracking tools that help you monitor your actions and milestones. Consider sharing progress reports or updates with your accountability partner to enhance transparency.

6. Create Deadlines and Milestones: Establish deadlines and milestones to break down your goals into smaller, achievable tasks. Set specific dates for completing each task and hold yourself accountable to meet those deadlines. Share these deadlines with your accountability partner to increase the sense of responsibility.

7. Public Commitment: Publicly commit to your goals and share them with others, such as friends, family, or colleagues. This adds a layer of accountability as you have a larger audience who can support, encourage, and hold you accountable for your progress.

8. Celebrate Achievements: Celebrate your achievements and milestones along the way. Recognize and reward yourself for completing tasks, reaching milestones, or overcoming obstacles. This positive reinforcement enhances motivation and encourages continued progress.

9. Reflect and Adjust: Regularly reflect on your progress and assess whether your accountability structure is adequate. Evaluate what's working and what needs adjustment. Be open to feedback from your accountability partner and make necessary changes to improve your accountability structure.

10. Personal Responsibility: Personal responsibility is at the core of any accountability structure. Take ownership of your goals, actions, and outcomes. Hold yourself accountable for following through on your commitments and staying dedicated to your goals, even when faced with challenges or setbacks.

Creating accountability structures provides a framework for staying focused, motivated, and committed to your goals. By leveraging the support of an accountability partner, setting clear expectations, utilizing tools and systems, and taking personal responsibility, you can enhance your chances of success and achieve your desired outcomes.

Chapter 9

Maintaining Balance and Well-being

Balancing Work and Personal Life

Balancing work and personal life is essential for well-being, happiness, and success. It involves effectively managing your time, setting boundaries, and prioritizing activities contributing to your professional and personal fulfillment. Here are key points to consider when it comes to balancing work and personal life:

1. Define Your Priorities: Identify your priorities in both work and personal life. Reflect on what truly matters to you and what brings you joy and fulfillment. This will help you make conscious decisions and allocate time and energy accordingly.

2. Set Boundaries: Establish boundaries between work and personal life to avoid blurring lines. Determine specific times when you are fully dedicated to work and other times when you prioritize personal activities, relationships, and self-care. Communicate these boundaries to your colleagues, clients, and loved ones to manage expectations.

3. Manage Time Effectively: Practice time management to optimize productivity and create space for personal activities. Set realistic goals, prioritize tasks, and utilize tools and techniques such as to-do lists, calendars, and scheduling to ensure that work and personal commitments are given adequate attention.

4. Delegate and Seek Support: Learn to delegate tasks at work and seek support when needed. Delegate responsibilities to capable colleagues or outsource specific tasks to lighten

your workload. Similarly, lean on family members, friends, or hired help to share personal responsibilities and create more time for self-care and leisure.

5. Practice Self-Care: Prioritize self-care activities to maintain physical, mental, and emotional well-being. This can include exercise, meditation, hobbies, spending time with loved ones, or engaging in activities that bring you joy and relaxation. Taking care of yourself allows you to recharge and be more productive in all areas of life.

6. Separate Work and Personal Spaces: Create physical boundaries between your work and personal spaces, primarily if you work remotely or have a flexible schedule. Designate a specific area for work-related tasks and separate it from sites dedicated to individual activities. This helps maintain a clear distinction between work and personal life.

7. Practice Mindfulness: Cultivate mindfulness to be fully present at the moment, whether at work or during personal activities. When engaged in work, focus on the task, and when spending time with loved ones or pursuing personal interests, be fully present and attentive. This enhances the quality of your experiences in both domains.

8. Communicate Openly: Foster open communication with your employer, colleagues, and loved ones about your needs, priorities, and challenges. Discuss flexible work arrangements, time off, and any concerns or conflicts that may arise. Effective communication helps in finding mutually beneficial solutions and maintaining work-life balance.

9. Learn to Say No: Be comfortable saying no to additional work commitments or personal requests that may

overwhelm your schedule or compromise your well-being. Prioritize tasks and activities that align with your goals and values, and politely decline those that don't.

10. Regularly Assess and Adjust: Regularly evaluate and reassess your work-life balance to ensure it remains aligned with your changing circumstances, goals, and priorities. Be willing to adjust, seek support when needed, and adapt your strategies.

Finding the right balance between work and personal life is an ongoing process that requires self-awareness, conscious choices, and periodic adjustments. By setting priorities, establishing boundaries, managing time effectively, and prioritizing self-care, individuals can lead fulfilling lives that encompass professional success and personal happiness.

The Role of Discipline in Overall Well-being

Discipline plays a crucial role in maintaining overall well-being. It involves consistent self-control, focus, and adherence to healthy habits and routines. Here are key points to consider regarding the role of discipline in overall well-being:

1. Establishing Healthy Habits: Discipline enables the development of healthy habits that contribute to physical, mental, and emotional well-being. It involves committing to regular exercise, maintaining a balanced diet, getting sufficient sleep, and engaging in activities that promote mental and emotional health, such as meditation or journaling.

2. Consistency in Self-Care: Discipline is necessary to prioritize and consistently engage in self-care activities. It involves making time for relaxation, leisure, and activities

that bring joy and fulfillment. By always practicing self-care, individuals can recharge, reduce stress, and maintain overall well-being.

3. Managing Emotions and Thoughts: Discipline helps in managing emotions and thoughts effectively. It involves developing self-awareness, recognizing negative patterns or behaviors, and implementing strategies to regulate emotions and cultivate a positive mindset. Disciplined individuals are better equipped to handle stress, overcome challenges, and maintain mental and emotional balance.

4. Enhancing Productivity: Discipline contributes to increased productivity and efficiency. It involves setting goals, prioritizing tasks, and following through on commitments. Disciplined individuals can better manage their time, avoid procrastination, and stay focused on their jobs, leading to greater productivity and a sense of accomplishment.

5. Building Resilience: Discipline fosters resilience, the ability to bounce back from setbacks and adapt to challenges. It involves perseverance, determination, and a strong work ethic. Disciplined individuals are more likely to stay committed to their goals, navigate obstacles with determination, and recover quickly from failures or setbacks.

6. Creating Balance: Discipline helps in creating a balance between various areas of life, such as work, relationships, personal growth, and leisure. It involves setting boundaries, managing priorities, and making conscious choices to allocate time and energy to different aspects of life. By maintaining balance, individuals can avoid burnout and maintain overall well-being.

7. Strengthening Relationships: Discipline contributes to healthy relationships. It involves practicing active listening, effective communication, and investing time and effort to nurture connections. Disciplined individuals are more reliable, dependable, and committed to maintaining healthy relationships, positively impacting overall well-being.

8. Pursuing Personal Growth: Discipline is essential for personal growth and development. It involves consistently following learning, acquiring new skills, and setting goals for self-improvement. Disciplined individuals are proactive in seeking growth opportunities, investing time and effort in self-development, and continuously challenging themselves to reach new heights.

9. Cultivating Long-Term Well-being: Discipline focuses on long-term well-being rather than instant gratification. It involves making choices that align with long-term goals and values, even if they require sacrifice or effort in the short term. Disciplined individuals prioritize sustainable practices that promote overall well-being over temporary indulgences.

10. Empowering Self-Control: Discipline empowers individuals with self-control and the ability to make conscious decisions. It involves resisting impulsive behaviors, temptations, and distractions that may hinder well-being. Disciplined individuals can make choices aligned with their values and long-term well-being, leading to empowerment and fulfillment.

Discover the power of discipline! It's the key to unlocking a life of well-being. By fostering healthy habits, managing emotions and thoughts, enhancing productivity, building resilience, creating balance, strengthening relationships, pursuing personal growth, and cultivating long-term well-being, discipline is the ultimate tool for achieving your goals. Don't wait any longer to start living your best life! Experience a fulfilling and purposeful life by embracing discipline, which can significantly improve your well-being.

Chapter 10

Overcoming Setbacks and Bouncing Back

Learning from Failure

Failure is an inevitable part of life, and embracing it as an opportunity for growth and learning can lead to personal and professional development. Here are key points to consider regarding education from failure:

1. Embrace a Growth Mindset: Adopting a growth mindset is essential when learning from failure. Instead of viewing failure as a reflection of one's abilities or worth, see it as a chance to learn, improve, and develop resilience. Embrace the belief that failure is a stepping stone to success.

2. Reflect on Mistakes and Missteps: Reflect on the failure and analyze what went wrong. Look for lessons, insights, and areas where improvements can be made. Be honest and identify any patterns or behaviors contributing to the failure.

3. Extract Lessons and Adjust Strategies: Identify lessons learned from the failure and use them to adjust your strategies and approaches moving forward. Consider what worked and didn't, and use that knowledge to refine your plans or actions. Apply the insights gained to make informed decisions in the future.

4. Cultivate Resilience and Perseverance: Failure can be discouraging, but cultivating resilience and perseverance is critical to returning. Understand that setbacks are a natural part of the journey toward success. Develop the mental and

emotional strength to persist despite failures and setbacks, using them as stepping stones to achieve your goals.

5. Seek Feedback and Support: Reach out to mentors, colleagues, or trusted individuals who can provide feedback and support. Their perspective can offer valuable insights and help you gain a different viewpoint on failure. Constructive input and guidance can assist in identifying areas of improvement and charting a path forward.

6. Take Calculated Risks: Failure often comes from taking risks, and while it may result in setbacks, it can also lead to significant growth and success. Assess risks, weigh potential rewards, and make informed decisions. Learn to step out of your comfort zone and embrace calculated risks that align with your goals and aspirations.

7. Adapt and Iterate: Failure allows you to adapt and iterate your strategies. Embrace the concept of continuous improvement and be open to making adjustments based on the lessons learned. Use failure as a catalyst for innovation, creativity, and finding new approaches to achieve your objectives.

8. Maintain a Positive Mindset: Adopting a positive mindset in the face of failure is crucial. Avoid dwelling on negative thoughts or self-blame. Instead, focus on the lessons learned, the opportunities for growth, and the potential for future success. Maintain a positive outlook and believe in your ability to overcome challenges.

9. Embrace the Journey: Understand that failure is not a final destination but a part of the journey toward success. Embrace the process of learning, growing, and evolving. Celebrate small victories and milestones, knowing that each failure brings you closer to achieving your goals.

10. Persist and Keep Going: The essential aspect of learning from failure is to keep going. Persevere through setbacks, remain determined, and stay committed to your goals. Embrace failures as valuable learning experiences contributing to personal and professional growth.

Learning from failure is a powerful catalyst for growth, resilience, and success. By embracing failure as an opportunity for learning, adjusting strategies, seeking feedback, and maintaining a positive mindset, individuals can extract valuable lessons that propel them toward achieving their goals and aspirations.

Reframing Challenges as Opportunities

Reframing challenges as opportunities is a mindset shift that empowers individuals to positively view difficulties, setbacks, and obstacles. Instead of seeing them as roadblocks, reframing allows individuals to recognize the potential for growth, learning, and new possibilities. Here are key points to consider when it comes to reframing challenges as opportunities:

1. The shift in Perspective: Reframing challenges involves changing how you perceive and interpret them. Instead of viewing them as negative or overwhelming, reframe them as opportunities for personal and professional development. See challenges as chances to learn, innovate, and discover new solutions.

2. Embrace a Growth Mindset: Adopt a growth mindset that believes in the capacity for growth and improvement. Embrace the belief that challenges provide opportunities for learning and development. Recognize that setbacks are not failures but stepping stones toward success.

3. Seek Learning and Growth: Approach challenges with a mindset focused on learning and growth. Embrace the opportunity to acquire new knowledge, develop new skills, and expand your capabilities. See challenges as catalysts for personal and professional development.

4. Problem-Solving and Creativity: Challenges often require problem-solving and innovative thinking. Embrace the chance to exercise your creativity and find unique solutions. Reframing challenges as opportunities encourages you to think outside the box, explore different perspectives, and consider unconventional approaches.

5. Building Resilience: Challenges test the resilience and inner strength. Reframing them as opportunities allows you to build resilience by facing and overcoming difficulties. Stability enables you to bounce back from setbacks, adapt to change, and persevere in adversity.

6. Strengthening Adaptability: Challenges often require adaptability and flexibility. Reframing challenges as opportunities helps you develop the ability to adapt to new circumstances and embrace change. It fosters a mindset that sees change as a chance for growth and improvement.

7. Discovering New Paths: Challenges can redirect your path and lead you to unexpected opportunities. Embrace the chance to explore new avenues, take different routes, and find alternative approaches to success. Reframing challenges allows you to remain open to possibilities and seize new opportunities that may arise.

8. Cultivating a Positive Mindset: Reframing challenges as opportunities promotes a positive mindset. It enables you to maintain optimism, focus on solutions, and approach difficulties with a can-do attitude. A positive mindset

empowers you to overcome challenges and maximize opportunities.

9. Embracing Continuous Improvement: Challenges provide a platform for continuous improvement. Reframing them as opportunities fosters a mindset of ongoing growth and development. Embrace the chance to learn from mistakes, iterate on previous efforts, and constantly improve yourself and your work.

10. Celebrating Achievements: Reframing challenges as opportunities allows you to celebrate achievements and milestones. Recognize and acknowledge the progress made, the skills acquired, and the lessons learned during the process. Celebrating achievements boosts motivation and reinforces the positive impact of reframing challenges.

Reframing challenges as opportunities is a powerful mindset that empowers individuals to approach difficulties with resilience, creativity, and a growth-oriented perspective. By embracing challenges as chances for learning, growth, and innovation, individuals can navigate obstacles more effectively and unlock their full potential.

Goal-Setting Worksheet

1. Define Your Goal:

What is your specific goal? Be clear and specific about what you want to achieve.

Write down your goal concisely and measurably.

2. Set a Deadline:

When do you want to achieve this goal? Set a specific deadline to create a sense of urgency.

3. Identify Your Motivation:

Why is this goal important to you? Identify the reasons why you are motivated to achieve it.

Consider the personal benefits, values alignment, or long-term impact of reaching this goal.

4. Break it Down:

Divide your goal into smaller, manageable steps or milestones.

List the specific actions or tasks to move closer to your goal.

5. Establish a Timeline:

Assign deadlines to each step or milestone.

Create a timeline that outlines when you plan to complete each task.

6. Assess Resources and Support:

Identify the resources, tools, or skills you need to accomplish your goal.

Determine if there is any support or assistance you require from others.

_____
_____
_____

7. Anticipate Obstacles:

What challenges or obstacles might you encounter along the way?

_____
_____
_____

Identify potential roadblocks and think about strategies to overcome them.

_____
_____
_____

8. Review and Adjust:

Regularly review your progress and assess if any adjustments or modifications are needed.

_____
_____
_____

Be flexible and willing to adapt your plan as necessary.

_____
_____
_____

Conclusion

In the dance of life, challenges emerge as partners on the stage. Yet, with a twist of perception, these partners can transform into opportunities. Like skilled dancers, we can learn to reframe challenges as moments to learn, grow, and innovate. Through this graceful shift of mindset, we discover resilience, creativity, and new paths to success. So, let us embrace the rhythm of reframing, stepping boldly into the spotlight of possibility. In this dance of challenges and opportunities, we become the choreographers of our extraordinary journey.

Milton Keynes UK
Ingram Content Group UK Ltd.
UKHW021304161123
432693UK00026B/1042